WHY DONALD TRUMP IN 2024

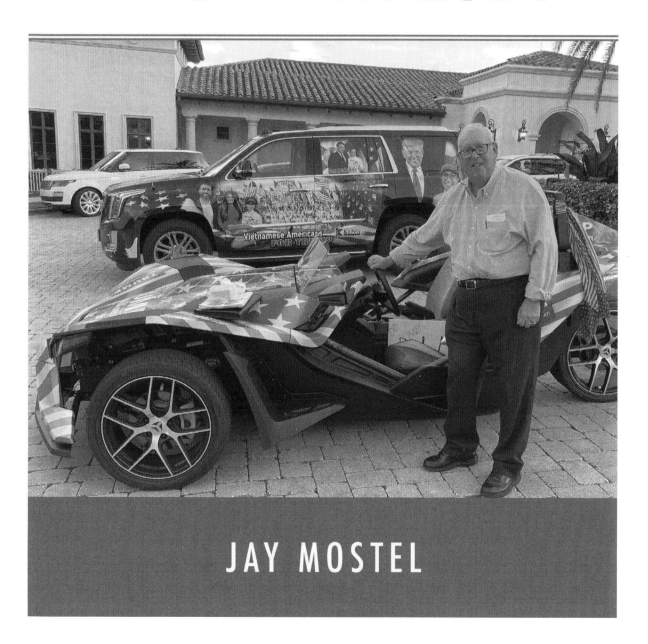

JAY MOSTEL

FOREWARD

Why write a book?

Since retiring 4 years ago, I found I had a lot of free time on my hands, especially when my wife Lonnie is either shopping, playing Mah Jong, water aerobics, watching her over 50 mindless and useless TV shows, cooking, cleaning or going to work. So, I wanted to accomplish something important to me. I couldn't care less about what others feel is important.

So, it became one of my "Bucket list" items. Others include, but are not limited to, cruising, making more CDs, seeing Donald Trump in Mara Lago, seeing Melania in Mara Lago, communicating with my dad somehow, get approval from my mom and that she doesn't think I am a gurnish (a nothing), volunteer at a Long-Term Care or Rehab facility and entertain the residents, design and complete my own personal photo album, travel to Israel, Australia, Wyoming, North and South Carolina, Graceland and most importantly, a safari with my grandson, Akiva.

The book thing began when I couldn't sleep at night. I was concerned and worried about everything-world events, personal problems. I made a list of potential Chapters and brought it to Gulf Stream Park to show my friend KP. This is a first for me. Forgive the bad taste, the "Three Stooges type humor", the Not politically correct statements and whatever else is offensive to you.

Enjoy the book!

CHAPTER 1

World War III

Two old friends, Jewish guys Yitz and Fritz were having brunch at the diner. They are both retired now and meet every Wednesday for brunch.

Yitz started the conversation saying "I think this President may start World War 3".

Fritz replies "Shoyn. What are you blaming him for? You know he is just a puppet. Besides, one man cannot start a war. What are you talking such nonsense?".

Yitz: "because he is so stupid and ignorant, he doesn't realize what is going on". Fritz says, "what do you mean? He is the President. He gets daily reports on what is going on."

Yitz: "the Chinese people gave the world this virus and started World War 3. Look at us schmucks. We have lockdowns, we have to wear masks, schools are closed to students, we can't go out of the house, everybody is fighting with one another, Democrats and Republicans cannot discuss issues civilly, siblings fighting with siblings, friends cannot get along. The whole society has gone crazy because of this virus that they unleashed on the world.

Thank God President Trump got us those vaccines in Warp speed, otherwise it would be much worse, we would all be dead from this. And that's what they wanted." Fritz is naturally shocked.

He responds, "How do you know for sure that China caused this? There is no proof of that."

So Yitz says, "It's been covered up by the Communists. It was intentional, I tell you and this guy Gowchi? I think he is the gang leader. He is covering up everything from the beginning, they should check his bank accounts because, for sure he is being paid off by those rotten Commies. And our stupid President is colluding with the Commies, beholding to China because his idiot son, the drug addict, is being paid billions under the table to keep his father quiet. So, China can do whatever it wants, unleashing more variants on us. This will continue until we are all dead from this. It's a biological war that we are losing and we don't even realize it. We are all schmucks.

We let the President off the hook. He should be deported to China, where he belongs. China can commit any crime they want with zero consequences and zero consequences for the President.

Fritz: "Again, tell me what Biden's idiot son has to do with this?".

Yitz: "You know his laptop is being held by the FBI and you know who is in charge of the FBI? His father! We will never see the evidence. So, the Chinese commies gave us this virus, the endless variants and they are laughing at what morons we are.

Fritz: "so what should we do, genius?

Yitz: "if I were President, I would fight back. I would react decisively. I would kill them all. Wipe them off the face of this planet. Once and for all. We have no choice. We are like sitting ducks waiting to be slaughtered. I say we should end it once and for all. You know my friend Howie? Well, he calculated that it would take about 100 hydrogen bombs to destroy China. It would take us less than a day and they would be gone. And that would just be the start. Kill billions of them. They think they're so brilliant? I say kill all of them, even the ones in our country. Round them up and kill them all. They are our enemy. And Fritz is bewildered. He says," are you crazy? So Yitz says, they are all over the place. They infiltrated our education system. They are in all the Ivy league colleges. These communists are brainwashing our kids, They should all be killed."

Fritz: "now you sound just like Hitler!"

Yitz: "what are you talking about? I am Jewish, don't insult me, you putz."

Fritz asks the waiter for a refill on the coffee. Estelle is listening to them and she comes over with coffee.

Yitz on a roll: "You know, we should wipe out Japan too. More out to destroy us, they started World War 2, We are idiots. What the hell was Hawaii doing in the middle of the Pacific anyway? We were just asking to be attacked. They are still laughing at us. They lost the war, so we gave them reparations and they destroyed our auto industry, our electronics industry. These Japs hate us. We should take them out too. How many hydrogen bombs you think we have?

Fritz has had enough

Fritz: "I think I know a good psychiatrist who can treat you. You are delusional. In fact, I think you need a whole team of psychiatrists. You think everyone is out to destroy us?"

Yitz replies, "No. Not everybody. Just the Chinese and Japanese people. Actually, anyone that doesn't look like us."

Fritz: "You're really worrying me. I need some more coffee - Estelle?

Yitz, my boy, you're really worrying me.

Anyone who doesn't look like us? What about Black people?

Yitz: "No not them. They are mostly like us. They work, share the same values for the most part. Except BLM. They are out to kill us. We have to take them out too."

Fritz: "So you want to kill all the Chinese, Japanese people and BLM? I think I don't want to know you anymore. Forget me for next Wednesday".

One last question. What about the Puerto Ricans? They don't look like us. You want to kill them too?"

Yitz had to think.

Yitz: "No, not the Puerto Ricans, they immigrated legally and for the most part, share our values, and are religious, they work hard and are citizens. They are not Communists. No not the Puerto Ricans, they are good baseball players and baseball is our national Sport, Baseball and Apple Pie."

Fritz is fed up and ready to leave, but he says we strayed off the topic, World War 3. He asks Estelle for the bill. Estelle, who has been listening to the conversation brings, the bill.

Yitz: "Well, many of my friends think I am a crazy person. I guess for good reason. But I am really a peace loving and friendly guy, A good neighbor with a lot of good friends, But I have to say Fritz is my best friend and I don't want to lose him like many others, mostly Democrats.

Yitz: "I am sorry, I don't want to lose you as a friend, By the way, you're not a Democrat, are you?" thank God he said no, He voted for Trump twice.

Fritz: "What do Democrats have to do with World War 3?

Yitz couldn't resist

Yitz: "Well, Biden and his stupid son are both Democrats and are getting paid off by China, so I guess indirectly, the Democrats are trying to destroy us.

Fritz: "So you want to kill all the Democrats too?"

Yitz said "Yup. I guess so. "

They both smiled and hugged each other

Fritz: "See you next Wednesday". Yitz loves his best friend.

CHAPTER 2

Election Fraud

It's 11 in the morning and we find two middle aged gay guys, Jeff and Steve, waiting for Jeff's mother, Sara Lee, to come out of the recently converted Unisex bathroom at the 3G's deli in Delray Beach. The place is packed as 3G's is a very popular breakfast place. It's hard to believe that a deli serves breakfast.

Sara Lee has been in the john for quite some time. Steve is hungry and complains to Jeff that his mother probably found somebody to bullshit with in the newly renovated Unisex bathroom. Steve has already decided on his order and is increasingly impatient. Sara Lee finally arrives at the table with a highly notice-able piece of toilet paper attached and hanging from her left orthopedic shoe. "Mom, can you please cross your legs so I can remove that piece of multicolored toilet paper from the bottom of your shoe?"

Sara Lee began explaining that a discussion pursued in the unisex bathroom between 2 young pretty girls that piqued her interest She said that one of the girls was upset about the odor in the next stall that was occupied by a man. "This person is not human", one of the girls said. The other agreed and said, "they could have converted one to unisex and made the other a Ladies' bathroom". During the girls' discussion, the man in the next stall continued to make animal noises and of course he began to chime in. "I will be finished soon, as soon as I finish crapping. I must have eaten something bad last night".

He continued, "I like this unisex idea." The two girls hear this schmuck and they leave. Sara Lee is still listening while going into the next stall. "I feel like I am at home with my wife nagging me to get out of the crapper. Nice to see 2 young girls in the same bathroom. Thank you, God, it's kind of enticing to sit on the pot and see 2 young girls." Sara Lee finishes up and leaves. He is still talking to himself.

Sara Lee starts talking to the boys about her problems at the voting booth when she went to the local church in Boynton Beach, District 21. Although she planned on voting for Donald Trump, her being a Businesswoman and was impressed with his business management skills and found it refreshing that he was not a politician. She said she was verbally abused entering. It seemed that a number of overzealous Democratic poll watchers that were urging her to vote for Biden followed her into the "private booth".

It wasn't so private. She said she was afraid that one of them would reach over and press the button for Biden and pull the curtain closed. So, she hurriedly pushed the Trump button and walked out fearing for her life or that she would be assaulted by a polling worker. So, she decides to order a Ham and eggs special with home fries. Her son Jeff orders his usual Potato Pancake with apple sauce and Steve orders his usual Tuna on rye bread and a diet coke. (The bread is freshly baked there). But Jeff says to his mother. "Mom, I thought this was a kosher deli you brought us to. You are kosher and you ordered Ham and eggs? Steve interrupts and says, "I guess it isn't." Jeff complains to his mother that he never saw her eat non-kosher ham before. She replied that she only keeps kosher in her apartment and for the past 5 years, she eats Traif {non-kosher food) when eating out. She deflects, "Steve, you always order tuna on rye. I think you can eat those three meals a day".

The discussion continues about the reports of election fraud. Jeff said that he heard about a truck driver in New York that transported a truck full of filled out ballots to Pennsylvania and that has to be illegal and fraudulent. The ballots were deposited at a predetermined location in Pennsylvania. The truck driver testified to this. Steve said that it was bullshit, that the truck driver made up a bullshit story and was not factual. CNN didn't report the story-only Fox News. Therefore, it was bullshit.

But Jeff cited another instance. He said that he saw with his own eyes again reported by Fox News, showing the Republican poll workers being told to vacate the poll premises to close for the night. But the Democratic poll workers stayed in the facility. The cameras then filmed poll workers at the same facility pulling a large box of ballots hidden under a table and counted by the remaining democratic poll workers deep into the night. And so on and so on.

Steve deflects by asking Jeff, why they don't call the potato pancakes "Latkes". He said it's a Latke, for God's sake. Jeff was on to him. He insisted the whole election was filled with fraud by the entire Democratic Party. That they cheated by systematically stuffing ballots all over the country after polls were closed. He said that in States that Trump was winning by a landslide, all of a suddenly, days later, miraculously, in 3 states, Biden wound up winning those states. Jeff blamed VP Pence for committing treason by certifying the election. Jeff proceeded to order 2 more latkes, this time with sour cream.

He said that Trump was right by asking Pence to send the disputed results in the 3 states back to the states for an audit and recount, which was constitutionally the correct thing for Pence to do. He said that the election was "stolen" and would be reversed by the US Supreme Court. Of course, this never happened. The Trump team and its legal team were unprepared for this battle.

Jeff had his latke wrapped to take home but left the sour cream.

CHAPTER 3

Did Communist China Start
a Biological War against the Entire World

The scene is the lobby of the Trump Taj Mahal Hotel in Atlantic City, NJ. In a huge couch, the hotel was frequently visited over the past 20 years by a group of friends named "The Airheads". Five couples from Oceanside Long Island that were mainstays at the hotel every month. The Taj Mahal Hotel, which was the Landmark of all the Trump hotels and properties in the Trump organization, is scheduled to be demolished in less than 3 weeks and the group, to a person is noticeably depressed as they walked through the mostly empty edifice that over the last 20 years, was filled with life and activity.

And now the Airheads are selecting souvenirs which were in the guest rooms, brand new, purchase for $100, $200 and $300 for a chair, a lamp, a table, Tv's mostly new Samsung, for $100 pre demolition sale.

Rooms, frequently filled by the likes of Mohammed Ali, the Clintons, the Zuckerbergs, the Beatles, Billy Joel and Christie Brinkley, etc. The Airheads usually stayed in 2 or 3 suites attached and usually left the connecting rooms unlocked for easy communication. Wendell, the comedian of the group enjoyed waking people up in the middle of the night.

Steve, the King of the Airheads, self- anointed, often played the slot machines all night and slept late in the morning. Jack, the most respected and intelligent Airhead generally complained about different ailments and conditions the whole trip. The 5 men spent the days walking the boardwalk and feasted with the wives at the various restaurants. Their favorite restaurant was the New Delhi Deli off the lobby and near the walkway to their second favorite hotel, Showboat.

The husbands often took a walk on the Boardwalk all the way to the Tropicana Hotel, having beers at the Hooters and watching football games and cleavage there. Mitchell often commented he thought he was in heaven.

"I remember when we first stayed at the Trump Taj Mahal the first week it opened. Time has really flown by. We were young then, now look at us", said Wendell. "AT SOME POINT THERE WERE 8 Trump Hotels in Atlantic City. I wouldn't be surprised if the Trump organization employed over 50% of the Atlantic City for 20 years. That's a lot of jobs created by Donald Trump. He sure is a job creator". Said Wendell. A semi-retired Nursing Home Administrator married to Melanie a retired nurse. She is very emotional over the demolition of their home away from home. She asks, "Hey guys, look at this beautiful table! It's a card table from the poker room. It's only $200. We could buy this and imagine that we were at the Taj Mahal playing poker at our beloved hotel."

Wendell, who is now sitting in the exact spot where he wrote a birthday song for Jeff called: He's an Airhead. Jeff is the same gay guy who was married now and divorced to Bernice. Bernice is bitter. Since their divorce she has been a recluse and their home in Great Neck is still filled with all of Jeff's stuff. But there is no room for his junk in a one-bedroom apartment. Jeff now cohabits with Steve in Manhattan. So, the junk remains in the house. Bernice misses Jeff even though he smells and has this obnoxious personality at times.

Wendell, who is Jeff's best friend for over 50 years since first grade and Wendell wrote "He's an Airhead" for Jeff- a classic to their poker playing friends. "He's an Airhead" employs a karaoke disc of Disney songs. This disk has the song "Be Our Guest" from the movie Beauty and the Beast. Wendell composed the tune in 3 hours in the lobby while passersby paraded through the lobby, most laughing hysterically at the cutting lyrics- "of all us little piglets, Jeff is the biggest".

Wendell wrote birthday songs for each of the Airheads. Mitchell is the favorite Airhead with the nicest disposition. He is married to Sofi, a ravishing redhead, a former 3rd grade teacher who also had a song written about her by Wendell. It was called "The Beloved Boatsmen" a song that described her characteristics to a tee. She is whacked beyond repair' She constantly yells at Mitchell as if he was a student misbehaving in her class.

The group often set sail on Jack's boat during the boating season. They would often be seen looking for "arans"- young pretty girls with the perfect figure. On the Atlantic City Boardwalk or beach in revealing bikinis with thongs. At times Mitchell would express his feelings remarking that "he wished he were that thong".

Sophie makes a comment that came from extensive investigation of things she heard on Fox News. Her favorite is Hannity about things happening in our country. "We are all helpless and are being laughed at by the Communists and we are not allowed to send our kids to school, they all have to stay at home and learn remotely by themselves, often with no social interaction at all. We all have to wear these N-95 masks all the time. The Communists started World War 3 by unleashing this virus and they won easily without a fight. Boy, we could really use John Bolton, the hawk. He would have led us in a war we could easily win with our extensive overwhelming military force. Instead, we have a weak President with a Military whose main focus is Political correctness and teaching Critical Race Theory to its soldiers.

And Bernice, unfazed and seemingly disinterested in Sophie's remarks says "let's go to the shwarma and steak restaurant for dinner tonight. They always give you so much food that I always have to take half home in a doggie bag for next day's lunch and put into one of the little refrigerators in the room.

There are hundreds of little refrigerators on sale for $100 each, so each of the couples buys a refrigerator as a souvenir. Edith, Steve's former wife, also a noticeable member of this group, has expensive taste. She is more interested in the high-ticket items like an armoire. "I will take that one for $600. It will fit in nicely upstairs in one of the many bedrooms. She built a mansion so that her 12 grandchildren who can all sleep over at the same time. Edith often can feed a small army.

Edith married Teddy. A lucky gardener who lives in the mansion with Edith. He gets to spend Steve's money. Steve is the wealthiest Airhead. He has a happy and confident personality. He is content supporting everyone, including Teddy. He is happy its someone else is with Edith and not him. He made most of his fortune gambling the Slots in Atlantic City. He is somewhat of a Folk hero. He had the uncanny ability to almost always win a lot of money at the slots.

So, everyone had a great trip. Eating substantially, bringing back souvenirs to last a lifetime, lots of fun, and Steve cleaned up as usual.

The Trump Taj Mahal was created to be a copy of the original Taj Mahal in India. How did he do it? Genius! With the large round Dome ceiling. A huge sky-scraper that was the Flagship of the Trump empire for 20 years.

The Airheads will never be the same. Changed forever. But they will always have wonderful memories with millions of others who stayed there and have great stories.

The Trump Hotels, where thousands of people worked for many years without a union. The Trump organization never used unions. Unions made the projects twice as expensive and often half as efficient. Specifically, the skyline of the Upper West side of Manhattan, built without unions is an embarrassment to Jerry Nadler, who claims to represent the people in that area. Mr. Nadler, however with the Unions' money and support, actively works against our President. The unions, sometimes labeled as Communist style organizations, led the impeachment proceedings through Jerry Nadler since day one of Trump's election, The New York

Post that day, instead of cheers and congratulations for our great President chose to feature on pages 2-5 Jerry Nadler's plan to impeach President Trump. So, this had been planned by the Unions and Jerry Nadler since way before day one of Donald Trump's Presidency.

That's it in a nutshell folks.

CHAPTER 4

Will President Biden Start a Civil War in the US?

The five Airheads are shooting at the Lantana Gun Range right off I-95 in Florida.

It seems that there is one thing they all have in common. They all have "potty training" issues.

These are deep long- standing psychological issues that have stayed with them since age 1 ½.

They have been close friends for over 30 years. I now introduce to you to Wendell (my favorite Airhead.)

He is the most talented, creative and handsome. He has the most success with women, except his wife. Mitchell (the favorite Airhead with the nicest personality), Jack (the most Bald Airhead who is technically the brightest of the group) and Steve (the self-anointed King of the Airheads. A true leader.) And last but certainly not least, Jeff (the bravest and most courageous) .

Jeff asks Steve, while he takes his turn shooting how many has he had today. It is now 11am. Steve puts up two fingers which indicates 2 bowel movements. This in itself is an indication where this chapter is heading. "Very good Steve" the group applauds as he continues his turn.

Wendell tells Steve that this is why he is the King of the Airheads.

Wendell announces that he has not used toilet paper in two years since he bought his cherished Bidet. He then takes his turn and gets 6 bull's eyes. And then Wendell calculates how much money he has saved in 2 years by not having to use toilet paper. Jeff reminds him that he should include an inflation factor.

They are reminded of the time when they were all sailing on Jack's boat into the Atlantic. Jack got lost. Jeff, who proudly had not had a bowel movement in 5 days, was bursting and has to go that second. Jack, in an effort to keep the boat clean, denies Jeff access to the head. They have a violent argument; Jeff succumbed and dove off the boat into the Atlantic Ocean where he completes the deed and is smiling. The other Airheads couldn't help but to notice little floaters right next to its rightful owner. They are laughing hysterically. Jeff eventually gets back on the boat to a round of applause. Please note the common theme of giving applause for taking a bowel movement.

A discussion pursues about the state of the country and how divided it has become. Jack says "We thought we had a unifier in President Biden following the Divider in chief, Donald Trump." Steve corrects him and says "we now realize that it is much worse than before. Every day, we become more and more divided". Wendell adds that "This is not sustainable. There needs to be a revolution". He then takes his gun and aims it at target and unloads all the bullets at the target. Steve turns to Mitch the sole Democrat, and says, "I just fired all your ammo".

Jeff claims that Biden is just a puppet that is controlled by the radical left wing of his party as well as Communist China that has the goods on him and his Crackhead son Hunter. Jack adds that "Hunter's famous Laptop from Hell has been in the hands of the FBI for over a year with no sign of doing anything with it. Fortunately, Rudy Giuliani made a copy of its contents that will be used at the appropriate time. Just this week a book came out called "Laptop from Hell." Supposedly with all the contents. "The media and the FBI will continue to suppress it." Then Wendell speculates "If they released it before the election, there is no way Biden wins".

Jeff corrects him. "That's not necessarily so. because no matter how many votes President Trump received, they would still have stuffed the ballot boxes with just enough votes for Biden to win." "But that's illegal." Jack claims. Wendell says that "Zuckerberg donated $419 million and supplied the Democrats with illegal boxes to dump the pre-filled ballots illegally deposited in the boxes. It was impossible for Trump to overcome that. They had unlimited funds to employ the most sophisticated and expensive methods to cheat. The laws only apply to those people following the law, not to the Democrats."

Steve continues his round. "This one is for Pelosi. This is for Schumer. This one for AOC. This one for Joy Reid. Next for the Cuomo brothers. Think I could take them both out with one shot?

Wendell says that what this country needs is a Civil War. Take our country back from these radicals. It's about time. He then aims at the ceiling. They all agree.

OK so let's go for coffee, they follow each other out carefully realizing that someone may be listening to them. Let's come back tomorrow. We need more practice to be ready just in case.

CHAPTER 5

Why NOT Donald Trump 2024

This chapter is something different. It deals with reasons why we should NOT vote for Donald Trump in 2024. Below you will find mini-reports on why he is a terrible person and was a terrible President his first term in office.

The country is divided, half love him, half would not vote for him. Of the half who would not vote for him, half of those could be described as having "Trump Derangement Syndrome". We will deal with that topic in the next chapter. These are the people, and you know who they are, who cannot avoid thinking and speaking ill of President Trump.

Here are samples of how they feel:

First of Four Submissions:

The Diabolical Genius of Trump by Wilbur Pentz

President trump did not create the animus that is prevalent in our country today. This friction existed before he was part of the political backdrop. He since recognized and capitalized on the clear and present hostility that existed. His "genius" was to leverage this feeling of alienation and hatred by serving as a symbol for those people who felt threatened by immigrants, minorities, the Far left and those democrats who had become Socialists. It is ironic that this self-described billionaire id the most unwavering supported and defender of the white working-class citizens that Americans have ever seen!

His base has been emboldened (see January 6, 2021 events) and empowered with anti-democratic attitudes and goals. This base has also taken control of the entire Republican party at this point- not because all Republicans support and agree with him- but because all these Republicans who were elected fear that the VOTERS agree with him. Most of his support comes from whites whose feelings of discontent emanate from the "Charles Lindberg, George Wallace and Pat Buchanans" of the party. According to political sociologist Martin Lipset, "authoritarian predispositions and ethnic prejudice flow more naturally from the situation of the lower class than that of the middle and upper classes." These people formed the basis of the White Citizens Councils in the segregated American south and Race-rioters in England. Lipset continues, "the working class groups have proven to be the most nationalistic and linguistic sector of the population. In a number of nations, they have clearly been in the forefront of a struggle against equal rights of minority groups and sought to limit immigration or impose racial standards in countries with open immigration policies." This ultimately describes a Donald Trump Rally.

Trump was originally derided as a "Fool" and not a politician. Well, this Fool won the 2016 Presidential election. He was well aware where he could receive support and where he had no chance of garnering any support. He correctly read the emotions of his targeted constituency and he preyed upon their fears and stroked their hatred and resentment. It was his belief that America was no longer "Great" because of the actions of the Black community, the immigrants, the "Mexican rapists", the Muslims or the Jewish community et al. His plan to "Make America Great Again" by catering to the bigoted emotions of people who felt disenfranchised by these minority groups and the Far-left liberals that were destroying American culture.

He realized that he entered the fray at a most opportune time. So, he and his supporters developed talking points that often led to violence and reckless behavior. Nonetheless, he supported and indeed defended these violent groups. "There were some good people and some bad people." He offered no solutions and like many other politicians made promises but did not deliver on those promises.

His topics of discussion were and still are designed as insight to his supporters and result in a frenzy, much like the famous demagogues. Of the 20th century. Trump used similar means at his many rallies to excite his base and focused his anger on his "perceived" enemies.

We should all remember learned his approach from George Costanza, who once said "It's not a lie if you believe it."

Jeff Doolittle, a successful Insurance broker says this:

The author clarifies an important statistic regarding the voters in America. The results of the latest Presidential election have, for the first time in history, been subject accusations of fraud, rigged election and other criminal steps to deny the prior President, his alleged crooked elimination in the Presidential race. Say what you will, but this country is split, nearly 50% are those who love him and his entourage, his executive acumen and frankly his long history of lying when it suits him. I, for one, dislike him for his lack of Legal knowledge and his inability to seek peace in this world of chaos and genocide.

Taking a photo-op with the Chairman of North Korea did not accomplish any international stability in the Korean peninsula. Sucking up to the Saudis did not benefit the United States or produce a reduction in our gas prices. Not caring a fig about our ecology or the dangerous changes in the World weather pattern received little or no attention from him. His immigration policies did little except to separate children from their parents. In plain and simple English, he ought to stick to his TV addiction, keep financially feeding his family, keep firing those on his staff that he felt were not loyal to him and continue to claim that he won the election even though he in fact lost the popular vote by over 8 million.

It doesn't take a genius to see that Donald Trump loves Donald Trump. He promised to submit his Tax filings. Keep waiting folks. His accounting firm threw its towel in and resigned due to a few million dollars of errors on his part. Those that admire him don't seem to care about his morals, his history of philandering is evident… but "what the hell? What's the big deal about screwing a few hundred women? He has plenty of lawyers to handle their grievances- a new meaning to "The Art of the Deal".

His school record is conveniently unavailable. His father dumped him into a Military Academy. Why? He was anything but an A student. He was then, as he still is today, a money hungry, ignorant bastard. He needed the discipline that wasn't provided to him at home. There must be hundreds of other severe financial indiscretions, all documented and attested to that should have disqualified him from holding any public office, no less the Presidency.

And finally, he and he alone spearheaded the January 6th debacle in the Capitol with the planning of his cohorts. The KKK, the Qanon, the White Christians and all his Republican crackpots that could carry a gun, a club or a gas cannister. He had the crass to sit on his fat ass and watch it all on TV, saying nothing and enjoying it. Our Leader? Yours perhaps- not mine! And what about the deaths of our brave Capitol police? Over 250 of them injured during the insurrection. There was not a word out of his mouth to attempt to halt the carnage that day. To support the notion that it was a mere "gathering of Patriots" who were ready to hang Vice President Pence- are we so gullible? His support of White Supremacy groups in Charlottesville and the killing of a demonstrator, the march by bands of neo-Nazis that shouted out anti-Semitic slogans.

Mr. Trump had the audacity to explain to us "there were good people and bad people on both sides". He learned absolutely nothing from history. Sorry pal but there are "No Good Nazis".at any time. You are a disgrace to your Republican party as you have attacked the Democratic process, spelled out clearly in our

Constitution, a document that you never read or understood. So much for your intellect!

And finally, you are responsible for the deaths of over 900,000 Americans because you did not have the guts to address the American people and mandate medical standards immediately upon being informed by the top scientists of its deadly implications.

You screwed the Business world royally, before your inauguration and even more so after your election. Remember Trump University? Trump Golf membership? And hundreds of more schemes.

As to the next election in 2024, sorry. You do not get my vote. Not now, never. Nor will your right -wing Senate myopic camp followers. Watch your back Mr. Trump. Some radical patriot might want to even up the score by feeding up your arteries with a few more fatty hamburgers. While you recount for the umpteenth time that Trump, you hump, LOST THE FRIGGIN' ELECTION.

The Declaration of Independence, July 4, 1776 states "He has excited domestic insurrections amongst us whose known rule of warfare s an undistinguished destruction of all ages, sexes and conditions".

And finally, to quote HL Mencken in the Baltimore Evening Sun, July 26, 1920 "As democracy is perfected, the office of the President represents, more and more closely, the inner soul of the people. On some great and glorious day, the plain folks of the land will reach their heart's desire at last and the White House will be occupied by a downright fool and a complete narcissistic moron."

The author probably did not think it would take 96 years to prove the accuracy of his words.

And Jerry Seidenfeld writes:

Many of my friends, for who I have tremendous respect and admiration, disagree on just about everything regarding Donald Trump. They are bothered when I say that Mr. Trump (notice he says Mr. Trump and not President Trump. Even ex-Presidents are given the respect and keep the title after they have left office) past questionable behavior and language as well as certain business decisions that he made disqualify him from ever leading the country. Some go so far as to say that he should be prosecuted and be imprisoned for some of those decisions.

I have tried to explain to them that in the real world a President needs to be tough with our enemies, especially those who don't play with the same set of rules as we are always expected to do. There are very bad actors in the world who should not be treated with respect because they don't respect us.

For instance, China, Islamic Terrorists, Russia and others should understand that the US is more powerful than they are. My friends argue that this approach and Trumps' lack of political and military experience has made us a pariah on the world stage and the laughing stock of the entire world. They say he is nothing more than a bully who talks tough but does little to back it up.

They also point out that Trump seems to cozy up to both Antisemites and White Supremacists in this country. This too, they feel makes him not tough, but a closet bigot. They believe that a person who is unwilling to condemn these kinds of people should be removed from office and should never be trusted to run the land of the free.

Cherna Sheindel from West Hempstead, Long Island says the following:

Just look at how great Trump Made America!

He spent his whole time in office insulting other world leaders without regard for human decency. He gave his whole family some of the highest paying jobs there are, taxpayer jobs, regardless of the fact that none of them had any qualifications at all except for the "Trump name".

He allowed the virus to invade America. Instead of closing international travel to America. The only consideration he had was for the economy because he is a business man, not a politician. He gave no consideration to the number of lives that would be lost and the lasting illnesses of those who survived. And then his economic considerations backfired because the economy hasn't been in such bad shape for a long time. The people were so desperate to get rid of him that they voted into office an elderly senile man who cannot even finish a sentence.

Then he showed the world how great he was by being a sore loser and tried to start a Civil War at the Capitol.

And so on.

CHAPTER 6

What Is Trump Derangement Syndrome and What Can be Done?

Yitz and Fritz are having a whole pizza at Park Ave Pizza in Queens, the best pizza in Queens.

They are reading the manuscript called "Why Trump 24".

Yitz says that his mom took him to a Trump rally in West Palm Beach at the Airport Hilton last week and that Newt Gingrich was the Keynote speaker. Yitz said he was ok but his mother was in love with Gingrich and was crying when he spoke. Really? Said Fritz? "Who is this guy? Yitz says, "He is this really old guy who thinks he knows everything and for some reason the whole audience of about 1,000 people applauded after every sentence. He was like a God to them. It was part of this Trump Cult bullshit, but it was fun." So, Fritz asks him what he talked about. Yitz says, "I have no idea but somebody asked him as question that sounded interesting." Fritz says "What was the question?' Yitz responds, "what do I do when a close friend who hates Trump and spends his whole day and night rambling why he hates him? How do I talk with this person?" So, Speaker Gingrich (see they call him "Speaker" not Mr. Gingrich. He was the Speaker speaking that night but that wasn't it. He used to be Speaker of the House of Representatives a million years ago. You know the same job that Nancy Pelosi has now, God save us)

Replied that "You don't talk to him. Let him carry on. Don't argue with him or listen to him. That person belongs in a Mental Institution. Leave him alone. Get other friends that are not crazy."

"Wow. He really said that?" replied Fritz. So, a discussion pursued about what to do with such a person that there seems to be millions of in the country.

Well, Yitz says, my mom, who is a relatively bright person, a College Professor in Behavioral something, says that there ought to be a clinic called "Trump Derangement Syndrome Institute" where this disease can be treated. Actually, there should be thousands of clinics opened all over the country and parts of other countries too. So, Fritz responds, "What? What is she talking about? ". Well, she says "you start with one, then another one, then another one—plenty of crazies out there!" So, Fritz says, "and what is done in these places?"

"Well, she says each one should hire a Medical Director, and he would hire about 100 staff including a Director of Psychiatry and about 20 psychiatrists that are specially trained in this disease."

"And each patient with this diagnosis which has spread across the country, would be assigned a team of such specialized psychiatrists to develop Care plans for these mentally deranged patients."

And then in a matter of a few years, we can be rid of this terribly disruptive and growing disease, perhaps in our lifetime." Fritz says, "you mean like COVID?" Yitz says his mother said it is much worse than COVID. "So maybe a vaccine can cure this. Fritz says.

So Yitz kids around and replies, "Wouldn't it be a pip if President Trump gets the Pharmacy companies to develop this vaccine? And he can call it the "Trump Vaccine for Trump Derangement Syndrome?"

"So, we can talk to President Trump about this idea. You know that's how brilliant ideas come about, from two schmucks like us," You mean like Facebook?" "Sort of, because this is much more important. Here you are fighting a terrible disease. What does Facebook do compared to this?"

Interesting. Let's go for coffee.

CHAPTER 7

Capitalism vs. Communism

Two teenage cousins, Cal and Sharon spend about a half hour hiding from the rest of the family at a mostly boring Thanksgiving dinner at Aunt Rose's house in Long Island. Aunt Rose lives alone since her husband passed away at a young age. The cousins are discussing topics such as school, what they did in camp and plans for the next year. Cal talks about his summer working for spending money for school and possibly buying a car. She says she wants to save for a car but hopes that Popi will buy one for her. She didn't seem to be interested in driving lessons and got her permit recently. He said he was going up to Binghamton State University in Upstate New York, near where his dad, Adam works as a Real Estate manager. His dad is his best friend. Sharon says her dad is also her best friend but she loves her dog a little more. She has 4 siblings and Cal has 2. What they have in common is that they have the same grandparents, Grandma and Popi. They agree that grandma runs everything and Popi just delegates everything he can to grandma. They both live to spoil their grandchildren. Sharon and Cal have a friendly argument about which grandchild is their favorite. There are 8 candidates but they truly believe Popi, who is brutally and helplessly honest when he says that the "middle Child" has to be the favorite! because the middle child is the one that gets the least attention. There are two middle children in the two families. They had fun discussing that.

Aunt Rose pops her head in and asks if everything is ok. They both stare at her until she closes the door to give them some privacy. These two have the most in common. He is 18 and very handsome. He has done modeling. And she is 17 and drop dead gorgeous. Cal says he had just spent a week in Florida 3 weeks ago and had a great time fishing, golfing, walking the Boardwalk at the Green Cay Nature preserve and winning at the casino (first time gambling). Sharon said she and her siblings and mom just came back from a week at Universal Studios Park with Grandma and Popi and it was great too. Grandma and Popi live in Boynton Beach Florida and had to drive 2 ½ miles up to Orlando for the week. Sharon and Cal both show each other cell phone pictures they took in Florida and made fun of many of them. They do so get along very well and are close cousins. Cal lives in New Jersey and drives and Sharon, who lives on long island asks Cal to take her driving. He says he has to ask his mom, Jennifer.

Eventually the discussion turns to politics. Cal announces he registered to vote and just voted for the first time. Although Sharon seemed uninterested in voting or politics, she listened as Cal said he registered as a Republican. She replied "Uch, that's disgusting. You're a racist! They were getting along so well but Cal told her he was not a racist, that he has friends that are Black, Asian, gay and every type.

She wouldn't buy that. Why would you register as a Republican then? He tells her both his parents are registered Republicans and since he will be studying Business in College, he was more comfortable with the Republican platform. She said her dad was a Democrat and a Trump hater. And that all Republicans are racist. She asked what he thought about Climate change and that Trump doesn't believe in dealing with Climate change and that he doesn't care that people will die because of climate change problems. Cal doesn't seem affected. He says that

Climate change is bullshit. He said that climate is and always has been changing. No big deal. Why waste money and time on that bullshit?

He said that Popi was an active Republican and campaigned for Donald Trump. He belongs to a group called Tuesdays with Trumpsters. Popi took Cal to a happy hour on a Tuesday. He said they party every Tuesday. She again repeated, "Uch". It must be all white supremacists like Popi". Cal said that it wasn't true. Poppy's good female friend was a Trumpster, a black Muslim. She was dancing and singing with Popi that Tuesday. So Popi is definitely not a racist.

"I don't care. My dad says he is, so I believe my dad. She said her dad said that Popi has gone off the deep end with this Trump bullshit. Cal loves Popi and is proud of his political involvement. He also has inherited his musical talents. They both recorded and wrote songs and sang them. They also performed duets, mostly Jimmy Buffett songs. Sharon also recorded with Popi. Her best song was Aretha Franklin's "Respect". Everyone recorded with Popi. Even Sharon's dad, Stanley recorded a whole album of Ray Charles songs with Popi. Cal said that Popi didn't deserve being called a racist.

"Well, that's why the country is divided and families are divided". Cal continued, he asked Sharon if she knew the difference between a Republican and a Democrat. She attempted an answer but couldn't come up with one. So, Cal asked her, I hear you are a straight A student, I am only a C+ student". She says she spends a lot of her off time studying and is very competitive, like her dad. Cal says he is the same kind of student as his dad too.

Cal continued, "I will explain the difference to you between Democrats and Republicans. Let's say you get a final grade from a teacher- An A. And let's say you have a best friend that's not such a good student and she gets a C". Sharon says it's actually true. "Well, you're such good friends and you want to make your friend feel better. Sharon says, "what can I do for her? I would do anything". Cal replies, "and let's say the teacher had the ability to change a grade, up or down". Sharon is trying to follow the thought. "OK". So, you had the ability to request that that teacher reduce your grade to a "B" and at the same time increase your friend's grade to a "B" so that you both would have the same grade. Wouldn't that be great? Would you do that for her?"

Sharon thought for a minute. "Of course, I wouldn't. Why the hell should I? I worked hard for the A. Why would I settle for a lousy B?"

"Congratulations, Sharon. You are now a Republican! And the Democrats, the Communist party are now a party of losers.

And that, folks is the difference in a nutshell.

CHAPTER 8

Election Integrity - PCL

Here we are in January. It's 82 degrees at a Condo in Boynton Beach, Florida where a group of friends are gathered around the "Boynton Bench" named after the Beach, It is about 8 in the evening and there are several discussions among the 20-30 people about the events of the day. And the big event is undoubtedly the Condo election which occurred this past week. We are listening to Ben, who is a very handsome and elegant 77-year-old lawyer, who still practices law.

The group is hanging on to every word from Ben, who speaks so eloquently, albeit a noticeable lisp that is actually very attractive. Ben is giving the crowd an update on the events of the day and the status of the Election results, which are not yet finalized to everyone's satisfaction. To say the least.

It reminds us of a Seinfeld episode in Del Boca Vista with Jerry's father running for Condo Board President. In this case there are about 20 people running for 7 Seats on the Board. It is very questionable as to why anyone would even want to be on this Condo Board. Once elected, it is not only thankless, but Board members are generally targeted for a whole year by residents complaining about a myriad of items affecting their otherwise boring lives in sunny Florida. What comes to mind is the temperature of the pool. You can't please everybody, or in this case anybody. Why Board members should be criticized about the temperature of the pool is beyond me, but this is just one of a hundred such complaints a Board member must deal with on a daily basis,

Back to Ben and the election. Ben and Sarah, who are next door neighbors in the 350-unit development

Both won seats, Ben by one vote over Vic. Or did he win? Well, there was a committee of 7 counters, (notice the number 7 is an uneven number as exists all over this country). These 7 counters confirmed and certified, as required by State Condo Laws, the results. But something happened during the night and the next day which changed the results. And so poor Ben (why he is so upset about this is beyond me) is pontificating to the crowd what he was told by Mr. Coffee, an obviously unbiased spectator and self -appointed judge of the events dealing with the elections and all else. You see, Mr. Coffee is accountable to both the Board and the residents but ultimately to the Management Company that employs him as the Condo Manager.

Ben is furious. During the day following the voting, the Condo Manager was approached by one or some residents who demanded a recount as they claimed there was an error in the counting. The names of the so-called people demanding a recount are kept secret from all the yentas present. This doesn't bode well with the group. They wanted to know who complained to Mr. Coffee. I imagine there are 20-30 such groups of residents all discussing the same issues in different areas of the development all with different opinions and stories. The recount per-formed by Mr. Coffee and unidentified others resulted in a reversal and Mel was declared the winner over Ben. This all happened so fast that minutes following the results of the recount, the new Board convened and started planning their first steps as the new Board. And they themselves voted on who should be the President, Vice President, Board Chair and Treasure are. Which they promptly did and within the next day, Mr. Coffee sent out an e mail congratulating the "new Official" Board members.

You say these people should really get a life!

It ain't over till it's over, said Yogi Berra, a famous philosopher and baseball player and manager.

So, Ben reads a letter he composed to the Condo State representatives that says exactly what I just told you. He spoke to a representative in Tallahassee who told him that thy already discussed Ben's letter and decided to do an investigation. The main issue being that the initial counting and certification by the Counters should stand and the subsequent events were unconstitutional and that Mr. Coffee who was not a member of the Election committee, should not have interfered. While this is the consensus of the group around the Boynton Bench, arguably there are 20-30 differing viewpoints.

So, we will wait for the results of the State investigation. The poor State representative selected to come down to the Condo and interview people will be hounded by residents who all have strong opinions as to what the State decides and probably, whatever the decision, someone is likely to file an objection to the State Supreme Court.

Why is this important? Of course, it is not to 90% of the residents.

But is has an amazing similarity to the results of the 2020 National Elections where it was obvious by the end of the day's voting and the voting booths closed all over the country that President Trump won decisively. After all, a monkey could have beaten a candidate who hid in his basement in Delaware for most of the campaign.

The night following and the weeks following the initial tabulation, all of a sudden millions of additional ballots appeared, all for Biden, the eventual winner. Trump cried foul. But it was clear that his legal team was unprepared for this and were useless in challenging. In fact, the US Supreme court decided not to even take up the matter. This in itself is a cause for concern, because most Trump supporters, I dare say 70% of the divided country, believe the election was stolen illegally from President Trump and the president to this day insists to his many devotees that the results will eventually be overturned by the US Supreme Court. I for one agree that this the right thing for the Court to take up and argue. But 50% of this hopelessly deadlocked electorate disagree with me. So here we are.

A year later and things are worse, we realize, all of us, that the wrong guy won. He is arguably in advanced stages of Alzheimer's and cannot complete a sentence. Trump Rallies continue at record numbers despite COVID regulations with hundreds of thousands in attendance. Biden's approval ratings are just 20% and dropping each day.

This cannot continue for three more years. Something has to happen really soon, before the midterm elections. Which begs the question- What the hell do Trump and Biden need this aggravation for? Biden may wind up in prison and for sure, the Anti Trumpers would enjoy seeing him in prison, for what? They don't know. Biden has arguably played Quid pro quo with China, Ukraine and God knows who else with his crooked son making deals making the whole family rich but beholding to our enemies. Which result in our losing influence with many world leaders, especially our adversaries.

So, it DOES matter!

But does the Condo election really matter? HELL YES!

CHAPTER 9

Bye, Bye Face Masks

Two old friends, Fred and Wendell are walking down by the Lincoln Memorial in Washington DC.

Wendell is visiting Sid for the 100th time in their 70- year friendship. They were born 2 weeks apart and their mothers and fathers pushed their baby strollers together and were also close friends. They go back. They had similar upbringings, liked the same things, went on numerous vacations together and until 6 years ago, were on the same page on many things. Then something awful happened. Donald Trump won. Fred wouldn't talk to Wendell for 9 months. He was "healing". He needed time. Wendell was excited over the Trump victory. He became a Republican later in life. Fred, a staunch Democrat was not happy. Who knew this would be a problem? But it certainly was. Both families were concerned over the apparent break-up of a long-standing friendship. Their wives and families predicted that they will be ok as long as they don't discuss politics, specifically Donald Trump. Hard to do when he was in your face daily, tweeting all day and night. They both had two different sources of News, Fox and CNN.

So, they both put up with each other's' shortcomings and tried to discuss other things, family, financial, mutual friends, medical conditions, etc. Wendell now lives in Boynton Beach, Florida and maintains an apartment with his wife on

Long Island while Fred recently moved into a luxury senior citizens' coop apartment in Maryland and bought a condo in Ocean City. Fred moved from the Bronx where he grew up with Wendell, and married Liz, 50 plus years ago.

A discussion begins with Wendell exclaiming, "I can't believe that next week at this time, there will be another Insurrection," a protest planned by mostly Trump supporters (Trump has recently left the Republican party and started his own America First political party). Fred, who is on the opposite side of this Civil War of sorts, wants to know the point of this. He says it will be very dangerous and split us up even further. The main issue is the Face Mask mandate by the Biden administration, Trump supporters feeling that Enough is Enough. That they wanted to go on with their lives despite this awful COVID virus. They both agree and are not angry at each other anymore. Sid fully healed. The families and wives are happy together again. They are all Facebook friends now. Children and grandchildren are like cousins.

What are they going to do? They both own guns by now, for protection purposes, not to kill each other. Both plan on being present he next week, albeit on two different sides. But it will probably turn violent, they both agree. Fred and his family had learned to live with the restrictions like lockdowns, school closings, Zoom education and wearing Masks. Wendell never was accepting of the status quo and wanted life to go back to normal. Wendell explains his theory that Communist China, who unleashed this virus on us, in addition, used the Face masks as a means of dehumanizing United States Citizens.

He says "We are not humans anymore. We cannot see each other's faces; we don't talk to each other anymore. We are more like robots, going through daily routines mostly by ourselves. No socializing whatsoever, no get togethers, meeting for dinner, a show. Or even family get togethers. Those days are long gone and forgotten. And the chinks even sell us the masks we are wearing. We can't even produce our own masks". So, Fred, while he understands is more accepting of the new mandates and living conditions, "it's not so bad. We are used to the societal changes and the Masks. They protect us, all of us, from getting the virus and the variants. We have all learned to live with it and don't mind it."

Wendell disagrees "No we don't. I won't, screw this government that claims to protect us, while they are covering up their collusion with China and using the American people and our way of living to appease an adversary that wants to eliminate us, take away our liberties, our personalities, indeed our faces."

And so, it goes on endlessly, hopelessly. The entire country has the same exact issue facing the future. Which future do we pick? Can we agree? Apparently not.

They continue walking trying to avoid the obvious conflict. Wendell says he is not willing to go through another extended 9-month separation and that we will have to agree on a compromise.

If you and I can do it, the whole country can do it? Where is the Unifier, the guy who was supposed to unite the citizens of this country? WE are more divided than under Trump! Wendell said the magic word- Trump. Uh-oh. Both sides then retreated to their respected corners, a boxing term, to strategize the next move.

TO BE CONTINUED

CHAPTER 10

Trial of Gowchi

Ben and Wendell are sitting around the Boynton bench with an unusually small crowd of only 10 participants. The residents, all aged 65 and older, are locked into every word that Ben utters. Having lost the election and then having it reversed by the Florida Supreme Court, Ben is now regarded as the Genius of the PCL Condo.

This week's discussion is about what will happen to Gowchi, you know the guy who allegedly was the guy who was responsible for the leak in the lab that created the awful virus that killed millions, including the President and Vice President of the United States. Nancy Pelosi is currently our new President.

Ben is laying out the Prosecution's agenda against Gowchi for the upcoming trial to begin next week. He says that it starts with money. Follow the money. He says that the trial, which is taking place in a Military Court in Georgia will start with showing how Gowchi was the highest paid worker in the Government, including the President. Hard to believe. It goes into a history of Government jobs in Government, ending with the NIH, National Institute of Health. They will exhibit many bank accounts in Gowcji's name, the most damaging ones are the Chinese accounts in Chinese banks under his name.

Wendell then says he can't believe it and if it is true, that is terrible and that Gowchi is really an idiot. Ben says that they will show there are unidentified accounts with Gowchi as signatory in Chinese banks with many millions of dollars, presumably from Bitcoin transactions. So, Wendell says, "Why Bit coin?"

So, Ben says "because it isn't traceable, I guess".

Wendell, who can't believe it says that it has an amazing similarity to what Hunter Biden has been doing for the past 7 years and brings up the laptop. He says Pelosi is still hiding the laptop and since the President died that there is no reason for the FBI to produce that laptop. Wendell has like most Americans been a Gowchi Groupie taking his word and advice as gospel. He says, "We were all fools, duped by this Communist". Before today's events, he felt sorry for Gowchi for having to go through this embarrassing Witch Hunt and Public humiliation. Now he has changed his mind. Before today, he joined the many millions of Gowchi followers in blaming President Trump for everything and that he would probably testify against Gowchi.

So, Wendell asks Ben, "what else can they try to prove?". Well, "they will try to show what effects the leaked virus had on US citizens" Ben replies. The country has become a "Village of Faceless Zombies" This will be a term that will be used by the Prosecution to show exactly what Gowchi caused and is accused of being responsible for.

So, Wendell asks, "besides President Trump. Who will be the main witnesses?' Ben says that the Government will produce Chinese Lab workers, about 100 of them that will testify to Gowchi's involvement including the cover-up of the Origins of the virus, that recently were confirmed that it came from the very lab that Gowchi was overseeing and he was responsible for. That the Chinese researchers will corroborate the story which will do Gowchi in. Also, US Government officials will show that he misappropriated millions through various agencies to the Lab and that much of it went to line his already substantial bank accounts.

So, Wendell says, "what can he be charged with and what can happen to him?" Ben tells him that the main charge would be treason which if convicted, is punishable by death by hanging publicly, like the wild west. "Ant thig else?" Ben tells him that he would also be charged with Second degree murder of Millions of US citizens, including the sitting US President and Vice President. That this is also punishable by death, but not public hanging.

"Very interesting. Want to have some coffee?"

CHAPTER 11

Bankruptcy and Inflation

Morty and Jerry are sitting on the dock of the bay (great song) in Miami at the Cruise Ship terminal. They both live in the same condo in Boynton Beach.

Jerry just took a job as a waiter on a cruise ship that is sailing shortly today. He has no experience in this work. The ship is supposed to sail for a week in the Eastern Caribbean. Morty asks his friend why he is suddenly becoming a waiter after running a successful gym for 15 years. Jerry replies "well the pay sucks but the trips are terrific, I hear. My business went bankrupt last week and I can use some money to feed my family. Luckily, I got rid of all my debts last month when the Gym went bankrupt."

"Oh my God Jerry. I didn't know that things were so bad. How did it happen?" Morty inquired. "Well, it was this God-damned inflation. It started when expenses were higher than the monies coming in. I got hit from both sides. As costs kept rising due to inflation, at the same time, customers couldn't afford to pay. In the beginning of the end, I ignored the signs, but every month it just got worse until my accountant insisted that bankruptcy was the right way to go to pay off all the debts."

Morty then corrected his friend saying that the debts were not really paid but just forgiven. The people who trusted you all these years just got screwed." "Yeah, I guess and some of them had to go bankrupt themselves. Sounds like it's becoming an epidemic-one bankruptcy leading into another.

Well, the price of gas quadruples in places since this asshole became President. The schmuck shuts the Alaskan pipeline killing thousands of good jobs leading to shortages in the supply of gas which increased prices of gas and before you know it, people cannot afford to live."

"So, it is not just businesses. It's families and households that are affected."

"Yes, what time does your ship sail?"

"In about an hour. It's a good thing I am able to escape to the islands. And to tell the truth, I couldn't afford to be a passenger. And when I booked this cruise, I charged it but then had to cancel as a passenger because my credit card debt was so out of control. So, I decided to apply to work on the ship instead. I was lucky to be hired at all. I happened to know one of the entertainers, Kenny Vee. He is also lucky to have a job. This ship did not sail for over a year. Kenny said his accountant advised him to go bankrupt which he did as well."

"What about you, Morty?" "Well, I can't afford to go cruising anymore. My credit card debt is also unmanageable. I cannot control my wife's spending. It is like a sport. So, I had to resort to menial work to try and pay off my balances in the credit card. That's why I am here-to look for some day work, day by day." "Well, perhaps you should consider personal bankruptcy. You only owe banks and they have plenty of money and can write your balance off, no problem.' "But I don't think bankruptcy is the answer because it would not stop my wife from spending more than we have. So, we would probably go bankrupt every three months."

"Marty, you really don't know that it doesn't work that way-it's a one-shot solution. To be approved by the IRS, you must prove that you can sustain yourself.

"And what about Donald Trump? Didn't he go bankrupt several times? I know he is very wealthy even after going bankrupt." "Yes "but he always had a plan, including with other businesses. You know that all the buildings he built he usen no union helpers. He was able to cut costs by more than 50%. "

"Really? That sounds pretty smart. So, when he went bankrupt and plenty of his workers would also go bankrupt. Pretty soon the whole country could go bankrupt."

"It already is." Says Jerry. By the way, Trump. Does he have any job opening for me?"

'Well, I think they are over-staffed, but the good news is that the major competition went bankrupt last month so all the workers came here. But it also doubled our business. But I will find out if there are any openings for you."

Thanks Buddy. Regards to the Mrs. You too Marty. Be well.

CHAPTER 12

BLM

I know what you're thinking. You think there is a chapter on the radical left wing group terrorizing America. Well, you would be mistaken. It stands for Ben, Larry and Me. Ben is the 80- year -old genius who is the main character in the "Tales of the Boynton Bench", and Larry is a frequent visitor to the bench. He is a House Contractor who literally lives with many of the unmarried women in the condo, a Don Juan of sorts who goes from quad to quad to at times a villa, servicing these ladies. All of them very happy just to have a share of Lenny. Larry fixes things like plumbing problems, minor electrical problems, Garage door openers, barbecues and TVs. A man of many talents. Especially in the bedroom, where his expertise is the most needed and appreciated. And Me, that would be me, Wendell, one of the main characters of the Condo and this book. Wendell has lived in the condo for 12 years with his adoring wife, who will be nameless for obvious reasons. Ben has been there for about 10 years with his wife, who also will remain nameless for the same obvious reasons.

The Boynton Bench is usually surrounded by 10-20 condo residents who discuss the events of the day. Much of the time the events include Condo elections, pickle ball championships, golf heroics (broke 120 yesterday but only on the first 9 holes), and many times a discussion will involve the latest episodes of perversions involving Lenny and a variety of his female companions. Actually, the men, at times have come to appreciate Larry as well because they enjoy it when their wives are happy and not spending the days yelling at them.

And so, Ben and Larry and me, Wendell have become very close. The other residents around the Brazil Bench have no clue as to why this threesome is so close. But Ben and Wendell have come to appreciate Larry's talents, mainly because Larry is handy, which, as most husbands, they are not, but also because their wives are happy when Larry is around. Ben and Wendell are happy to pay Lenny at least double the bill that Larry gives to their wives.

Ben does a lot of traveling, the most recent is for clients In Italy. When he leaves on his frequent business trips, his trusting wife gets lonely and often calls Larry to fix something. Ben is very happy to match the bill provided by Larry and considers it a well-earned "tip". A little pun about Larry's tip.

And Wendell, who while 5 years younger than Ben, doesn't travel but is very active with the Republican party. He was recently elected for a 4 -year term as the Republican District Leader for the District they all live in. This obsession, incudes weekly meetings, planning of Political events, such as elections, weekly participation at Trump rallies on Woolbright and 95 where you will often see Wendell, flag in hand yelling at the ongoing traffic about Biden or some local yokel. There are frequent Happy Hours, poll watching trainings, golf tournaments for Political candidates, dinners, mostly without wives, and so Wendell's wife also becomes very lonely and also requires her Handyman to fix something and so Wendell is very happy to pay Larry double the invoice, in cash of course, so Lenny doesn't have to pay taxes on it.

And the three are happy Conspirators often seen meeting on the Boynton Bench. This week's discussion revolves around the obvious neglect by the FBI, law enforcement and Media of BLM activities such as burning police cars- no one gets arrested, burning down cities and businesses, anti -white protests, and killing of Police officers. New York Post has daily headlines of such brutality but none of the other media outlets report on it. They purposely ignore it as if these events never occurred. Crime is soaring as well as the bank accounts pf this Terror group. The group is synonymous with the Democratic Party and there is a Quid Pro Quo in that monies raised by the Democrats wind up in BLMs bank accounts and vice versa, Much of what is raised by BLM is donated as campaign contributions for Democratic candidates. And so, this cycle goes unreported by the Main Stream media outlets and everybody seems very happy with the status quo. Except for the victims of these "Hate Crimes". They are not happy and are assisted by the growing number of "go Fund Me" organizations that help these victims.

Lately, these "Go Fund me" organizations have decided to divert funds to organizations of their choosing and not the ones set up to help the victims. This is the discussion of the day.

It is 2 in the afternoon and the two wives are busy playing Mah Jong, an activity involving no movement, no brain skills and little or no spending. The men are happy when the wives are occupied with Mah Jong. They are not being yelled at. This could happen 10-12 times a week. And there are so many games in the condo. They are hard to keep track of. And so, there is a Mah Jung Coordinator. And guess who that is. It has to be someone with a lot of free time and an affinity with the women. You guessed it- Larry! Larry is the Mah Jong coordinator of the Condo. Each condo in Florida has a Mah -Jong Coordinator. Keeps everyone happy.

So, Larry says, "what can be done about these Terror organizations?" Wendell says, "identify the leaders, follow the money, round the entire BLM organization up, arrest them and prosecute every single one of them." To which Ben says, "do you understand what kind of resources are needed to do this, how many lawyers, support staff are needed to accomplish what you are saying?" so Wendell says, "Once you identify the leaders, you don't really need as much, get them and the whole organization would be leaderless, without the support monies to pay the BLM staff, they would disappear." Larry, while interested is still opposed to this.

"This organization is in cahoots with the Democrats, the Media and much of the population." Says Larry. Wendell says, "Round them all up too".

"So, "round up the Media organizations, the Democrats, the BLM leaders and some of the citizens defending this organization?" Yes, but that is just the start. So, you are pushing for a movement.

Yes. Larry, his eyes bulging has to excuse himself. "Excuse me guys, I have to go over to Carmen and Guy before Guy comes home to fix something".

See you tomorrow.

CHAPTER 13

Mike Pence - Devil or Angel

Two old friends, Norm and Wendell are walking around the PCL circle- one time around is one mile. A planning genius must have figured that out. They generally walk daily at 7:30 in the morning, depending on doctor appointments, therapy appointments, wives' needs and the weather. These two have been doing this for over 25 years since they moved together down to Florida from up north. There are about 50 or so other such couples. Today's conversation turns to Mike Pence, the former Vice President, and recently a hot topic for Senior citizens all over Florida. There are many different opinions on whether he is a great politician or a traitor to the President.

Norm and Wendell are on different sides of the controversy. Norman says that he is the most decent, loyal and honorable person in the Administration. His recent labeling as "Judas" the traitor is unfounded and unfair. The issue of course is whether or not his judgment was correct in certifying the voting results when 3 states were so close and results presented by the media were premature, that they should have been sent back to the states for a recount and audit. "What was the hurry to certify?" Wendell argued.

Norm responded, "that was the date by law, that it had to be certified. And besides Pence is such a gentleman, a scholar, the most loyal person that could be counted on with grace and humility". Wendell disagrees vehemently. "He is a traitor to his country and to his President. He will go down in history as the single most important reason the wrong person was declared the winner. Although he wasn't involved in the "Rigging"- that was all the crooked democrats' doing, he caved in to the media pressure to certify quickly." Norm then responded, "you are wrong on both issues. The sore loser is looking to blame anyone but himself for the loss and the constitution is not clear on this issue. Pence studied the decision carefully and he knows the Constitution better than Trump". Wendell said, "Oh yeah? What about the Dominion voting machines? Wasn't it ultimately proven that the machine s could be manipulated and could switch a vote?" Maybe you are right about the software, but not about Pence. Pence made the decision before he knew about the software." You could hear him yelling a mile away.

Like many old -time buddies, there have been many such arguments, often about politics. Wendell then pulls out a small copy of the US constitution he stopped by his condo to get and reads a page that says that the Vice President should, when the results are challenged, send the voting results back to the states affected.

The topic is dropped at that point and they begin talking about their doctor appointments the rest of the week. Norman talks about his Physical therapy visit yesterday because his nose was broken. He told Wendell that a strange person smacked him repeatedly in the face over a political disagreement and not only was his nose broken, but two of his fingers as well.

That's all folks

CHAPTER 14

What's Next? Re-elect Donald Trump for 3rd time

So, it's Wednesday again and Thank God we are still alive. Biden did everything in his power to kill us all and all humanity. But, somehow we are still here ordering omelets.

Yitz and Fritz, remember them? They are still friends after 30 years. Estelle is still there serving them coffee while they decide what to order. This could take time. They have a lot of catching up. So Yitz says, "What do you think about the upcoming midterm elections?" Fritz says, "Are you kidding? It's gonna be a Red Wave like you've never seen. The Republicans don't even have to campaign. Do what Biden did. Sit in the basement and shut up for 3 months and watch the Golden Girls and Seinfeld". So Yitz says, how can you do that?" "Anyone that comes out of the basement and actually talks to anyone will probably lose their election".

So, Yitz says, "OK so there is a Red Wave, as you predict. Then what happens?" "Not much. Pretty much the same crap except we are still breathing. The Republicans are just as dumb as the Democrats. It will take 2 years just to regroup behind the real leader of the country, Donald Trump." Really, you think he is really running? You know Nicki Haley is getting a lot of exposure and a lot of people like DeSantis. And besides, isn't Trump too old?" So Fritz says, "are you kidding? Trump is a Kling On- he is not human. God created such a leader, ageless, like Moses to lead us out of this."

So, Yitz says, "Then what happens?" "well that's the easy part. Trump wins by a landslide. First he will learn from the Democrats and just copy what Biden did his first day in office- just reverse everything Biden did on day one. Then meet with all the World leaders assuming "all the bad guys are dead by assassination. Just the good guys and some terrorists that are still hiding." So not everyone is invited to this summit. "Where is this summit?". In Mara Lago, of course. Washington DC no longer exists. The prior administration moved the federal offices to Orlando. It is safer there and better weather. People actually enjoy working there.

"What about the mail, the Postal Service?" Bye Bye, post offices-sell the buildings, the planes everything. We have e mail and Fed Ex." "what about all the Unionized postal workers?" "Screw them all. They are deadbeats. Let them get real jobs. You know there are a lot of openings all over the country. The illegals are only qualified for some."

So Yitz says, anything else?" That's only the beginning boychick. Next the second week, start constructing the 1,000 Trump Derangement Clinics all over the country." Yitz suggests. "You were really serious about that in Chapter 6?" "what, you remembered the Chapter? Shh. I am the author. I also go by Wendell." So, what should I call you, Fritz? Wendell? I don't know who you are anymore." "Well, I could tell you but I would have to shoot you. Should I tell you?" "Not sure if you're serious," says Yitz."

So Fritz continues- " You round up all the crazy communists, like in the McCarthy era. They will all rat on each other. You feed them lots of Cheese and Illegal Russian vodka for free. And you arrest them."

"Third week, scrap the Iran Deal. Give Israel weapons and everything they need to destroy Iran, Wipe them off the map. Exactly what they wanted to do to Israel." "Go on-you're on a roll."

"Open the gas pipelines, close the southern borders, build northern border walls into Canada- they are a major problem too."

"Oh and scrap the Green New Deal and arrest all those supporting it as traitors and for treason. Give them a prison with no power no electric no refrigeration, etc. Let them rot."

"It is still very important to drain the Swamp, including RINOs. This could take years. Establish a "Drain the Swamp commission to do it."

"And finally, appoint a new loyal chief of staff, someone no one has ever heard of or seen."

"Anyone you have in mind?"

"What about the guy who wrote the book, Why Donald Trump 2024? That sounds appropriate-who is that guy? We should find him. I hear he is very handsome and charming."

"I think it's Jay Mostel. Yeah that's it! Great idea.

See you tomorrow, Yitz.

ACKNOWLEDGEMENTS

Mark Levin- Who made me feel that any conservative person like myself, could write a book. He recently wrote American Marxism (what a title-can you imagine what that means? Our country is not just becoming a Communist Country, no freedom of speech or press) it already IS one.) It was a NY Times Number One Best seller for many weeks. It is the first book of its kind in a long time to be a best seller.

To all the Trump haters in Chapter 5- Thanks for contributing. You inadvertently agreed to supply me with reasons NOT to vote for Trump in 2024. I initially wanted to share with my readers as an alternate point of view. These people actually represent about 40% of the country. Don't quote me on that or anything else I wrote, Its complete fiction, a political satire, just my opinion. Since reading the essays, I realized how incurably sick half the country is- and that is why Chapter 6- Trump Derangement Syndrome was created. These 2 chapters were the only 2 that had some continuity.

To President Donald Trump, who at my advanced age, decided to run for President. He never did that before. And I never wrote a book before. What courage! Thank you for donating a Foursome as a raffle prize at the Kushner Academy dinner, that my daughter won and let me use. I used it twice! Took 6 friends instead of 3. Thanks for writing The Art of the Deal 35 years ago that was my recipe for being a good businessman, leader, manager of people in my jobs and a successful and productive career. He also gets little or no credit for employing half the Atlantic City populations in his casinos for 20 years. So many people who worked there should be grateful for the livelihoods in jobs created by Donald Trump. He not only won his first Presidential election but both elections. Everyone deep down knows he won over that disgrace Biden. We will find out when we least expect it, that not only didn't he cause the January 2021 event at the Capitol, but that he was framed by a plan by Nancy Pelosi, just like the 4 year Russian hoax. I believe the Supreme Court eventually will review and reverse the results of the 2020 election. I also believe that the Dominion Software creators will be indicted, for what I am not sure. But something that changed the outcome from an apparent landslide for President Trump.

My most important personal thank you's to KP, who at the same time I was recovering from strokes, so was he. We recovered together. At an advanced age, like me, he decided to make a documentary movie and spent the entire pandemic working very hard on a film, which will be out momentarily. He never produced a movie before. He and his crew make quite an impressive team. The movie is about the origins of Rock and Roll, featuring interviews and performances by legendary singers of our youth. With all that was going on with the movie, he somehow made the time to spend a lot of time with me and encouraged me to write this book. Sitting on the beach at Gulf Stream Park with me, I showed him a list of Chapters of the book, he said "this is good shit. Can you do this? KP, you are my inspiration in so many ways. You are my Mentor and you know it. So please keep on performing, but not such a hectic schedule please. We need you around a lot more healthy and entertaining years. I feel like your Sanchez in the Man of La Mancha by your side forever. You are "Good shit".

Norman B. Gilden, another new author of a book "Learning from My Experiences". Thanks for the meetings at Dunkin' Donuts and the advice you gave me. I have certainly learned from your experiences. Norm has been a colleague and friend for many years.

Lenny Getz, who although I just met recently in PCL, has also published a book, "From Broadway to the Bowery" about the Bowery Boys- I was a huge fan of their over 90 movies. Lenny is a genius. Although I only know him a few short weeks, I know we will be the best of friends for a long time. BTW since my strokes that affected my vision, I don't read. I have recently delegated all the books I would like to have read to my friend Dan Pollack, who reads 1,000 words per minute and an entire book in just two days if uninterrupted. He and his wife Maryanne moved in next door and since then have made my life more productive and enjoyable. So, thanks to Dan and to Maryanne for sharing Dan with me,

Back to Lenny- I pledge to help Lenny sell as many books as I can of The Bowery Boys. He is multi-talented. We are so happy you and Susan moved in so close to us. Lenny just completed our tax return. He is a CPA and I apologize for giving him a hard time during the preparation.

Thanks, most importantly to my family:

To Phil, my illustrious nephew, albeit a Trump hater. He correctly labeled this book a "Political Satire". Although in my visits to either the library or bookstore, I have yet to find that section. Thanks Phil.

To my mom, Esther, OBM, who passed away much too young at age 91. Mom said I was a "Chochum", an endearing term for a very bright person. However, I believe she said it jokingly. Either way, you were right. I am a chochum."

To my dad, Bill, OBM who really passed away much too soon at 72 from presumably a stroke, coincidently at the same age that I had my strokes. I learned that the term that describes this coincidence is "Elvis Presley Syndrome." Elvis died at the same age as his father of the same cause. Evidently, it's not as rare as one would think. Fortunately, or perhaps not, I lived and thrived. Dad was a hero in Battle of the Bulge in World War 2 and was also my hero. He was the inspiration for the hatred of Japanese people" I used in the first chapter referring to those people that sneak-attacked us at Pearl Harbor. He often warned us and anyone else not to trust the Japanese people. I used it to describe them . Alas, at the risk of being labeled a racist, which is far from the truth, to me they all look alike. Uh oh.

Was that politically incorrect? Who gives a shit. Besides, the Chinese people, possibly extinct by this reading, were called much worse. Chinks, gooks come to mind. Thanks to all the veterans like dad, who fought in our wars and often gave their lives so we can have a non-sensical Civil War in this country. I think my dad would be proud of me. Himself a musical talent (it runs in the Mostel family). I recorded 40 cds and developed a small but loyal fan base over 25 years and I was recently was elected to a four year term as District Leader for the Republican party and Executive Committeeman, the same position my dad was elected to in the Bronx in an overwhelmingly Democratic district. Coincidence? I think not. The apple doesn't fall far from the tree.

Thanks to Lonnie, my adorable and loving wife, who was not exactly supportive during this whole process. "you're working on that stupid book again? Stop wasting time! She is as beautiful today as the day I met her 50 years ago. Damn, I am old! Thanks for marrying me, clearly, I married up. Her favorite song that her mom used to sing was the Boll Weevil Song by Brook Benton- "Lookin' for a Home". It seems during the course of our marriage; we spent a lot of time looking for a home. I define a home as where your wife is happy and makes the whole family happy. Lonnie, you always made our homes enjoyable, despite my shortcomings as a home owner.

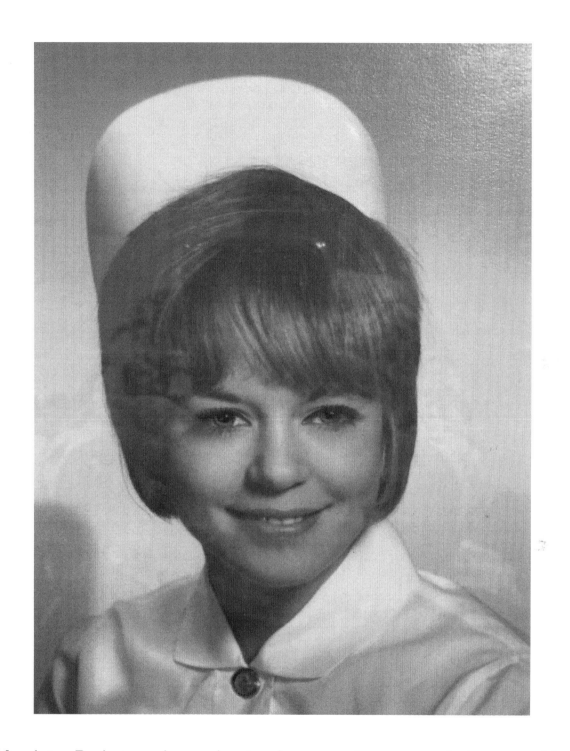

My sister Barbara, who understands me and my perverted sense of humor better than anybody. I often introduced her as my sister-she is an only child. That seemingly suggested that our parents favored her. Well, I can now see why. She is my favorite sibling.

My daughters Deborah and Meredith. Deborah for just being Deborah, always being supportive and understanding. I learn from her advice. And Meredith, who is a female mini-me, my clone, albeit more talented and sensitive. Thanks for helping me pick Lucy, the family dog for over 10 years. I only hope that when the book is done, it will include her illustrations. But if not, I love her anyway

This is my first shot at this and so the Thank you's are longer than the entire book. Who gives a shit? I am the author. Quoting Franz Liebkin in the Mel Brooks and Zero Mostel movie, the Producers who told the audience "I am the author and you will please shut up".

And so, finally, thanks to me- yes, I am the author, a tyrant of sorts, persistent through all the negativity and the doubts, being called a racist, a jackass, etc. I can't believe I finished whatever this is.

TRUMP ACCOMPLISHMENTS AND FAILURES

TRUMP ACCOMPLISHMENTS

1. Declared Jerusalem as Capital of Israel

2. Built US Embassy in Jerusalem

3. Assassinated 2 major terrorists

4. Developed a new Health Care system that failed by one vote in the Senate (McCain)

5. Appointed 180 new judges including 3 Supreme Court Judges

6. Reduced taxes for ALL workers

7. Eliminated gov't regulations which helped businesses

8. Stopped illegal immigration and reduced drug trafficking

9. Attacked MS13 gangs in Long Island and deported bad guys

10. Built Border walls to stop illegals from entering US

11. Boosted economy and created Stock market boom

12. Withstood illegal spying by FBI, other agencies and Deep State for 4 years

13. Reduced number of Deep State bureaucrats in White House and other Federal agencies, including the Veterans Administration. But couldn't Drain the Swamp

14. Daily Tweets created Transparency and allowed the President to interact with 200 million Americans on Twitter. He let subscribers to Twitter and media know what he was doing and what he was thinking and planning.

15. Withstood 4 failed attempts at Impeachment and was found not guilty on each attempt

16. Avoided war with North Korea, going into North Korea to meet with enemy.

17. Avoided wars in all parts of the world. No attacks on Americans during his Presidency

18. Imposed sanctions on our enemy, Iran

19. Cancelled terrible agreement with Iran made by his predecessor

20. Circumvented biased press and media by talking directly to American citizens

21. Made Pro American Trade agreements with China, Mexico, Canada and Japan

22. Reduced drug prices by speeding up FDA approvals of generic drugs

23. Created prosperity by creating 7 million new jobs in three years prior to Pandemic

24. Complete supports for Law Enforcement, Police and Military

25. Created Alaskan gas pipeline creating many thousand new jobs

26. Made us energy independent and no longer dependent on Arab oil (OPEC)

Failures

1. Didn't drain the swamp

2. Was not able to effectively manage the Pandemic caused by China

3. Did not get China to pay reparations for the Pandemic they caused the world

4. Did not fire terrible choices such as Jeff Sessions, who mistakenly recused himself causing the impeachment hoax of Russian Collusion now attributed to Democrat and Media disinformation

5. Was not successful in getting Vice President Pence to correctly send the Disputed states back to the States instead of the Media picking the Winner

6. Failed to get the Supreme Court to look at Election Fraud which would have changed the election result in 2020.

Drain the Swamp